And the soul may exist in the darkness until the spirit finds another life to live. It may sally forth into another body…and the soul may remain anchored in an unknown place.

A big thank you to my daughter, Melanie

and my friend, Julia

Cryptic Closet Talk

A Book of Poems

By

Kevan J. Cooper

Edited by: Kevan Cooper

Cover Design: Kevan Cooper

Publisher: G Publishing LLC

ISBN: 979-8-9876534-6-3

Library of Congress Control Number: 2023909341

Published and Printed in the United States of America

G

They came from nothing, a word ending in G, and that's

what they are. The nothing of G.

But they will become something; whose last letter is G -

and that's what they will be: their very own G.

They sent their boy to show you how to save yourself from

sin.

Their wolf got caught wearing a sheep's frock and they all

get pinned in a jin.

Not only have they all lost face - they have also lost their

case.

They have no cornerstone in place.

And no one else to blame.

They have no stool pidgin to lie for them; they end their

game in shame.

Hold Your Own

I told you no in the beginning.

I will tell you no in the end.

I told you no in my old age.

I will tell you no in my old stage.

So you get mad; acting vicious and vile

Still trying to get your way -

you can stay disappointed with a scowl on your face

Your efforts will not be rewarded today.

Stay empty, and hungry and dry inside;

And beg and demand as you do. Pay for your deceivers

disease

in the ways you believe; your lies are stuck with you.

You don't have any claim in my life and you will not get

what you need -

And the more you hang around talking debris, the more your nose will bleed.

I'm making you mad, and making you simmer to make your blood pressure rise

I'm teasing your temper and making you simpler to give you hate in your eyes

I will make you insane

And you bare the blame

For your talk - you yourself must refrain

House of Hate

It is you yourselves; your spouse and you

Who live in the house of the hate

You stared at us and hung yourselves

On a rope of envy fate.

Envy left you flustered

You couldn't cut the mustard

You tried to use your charm

But you only meant to harm

And that's what got you busted

No, you will never be trusted

Only You

You're the only one who knows - exactly - 'precisely' what

I am saying.

The only one who knows the difference between the

working and the playing.

Only you can pick out the unseen spot

The tick

The dot

The nuance

You're the only one who knows for sure

The meaning of influence

Truth From the Mouth of the Victims

Now all these things have been mentioned before,
but forgotten thru the course of time
They were told to leave from accosting someone -
but they chose to stay here blind

They come wagging their tongues, mouths wide open --
so many with something to say.
They cannot give us their blame.
They are red-face in shame and all their lies are on display.

We won't carry their burden or be their shield or help them
by being their crutch.
They will stab you in the back if you ever try to help them
They are cunning and treacherous
Too much

Such a pitiful effort they make trying to excuse their
mistake
Slithering around like a snake in the desert under hot rocks
they bake
But it doesn't matter where they are
- in the city near or the country far

All they do is deceive.
They're mad at us because we pulled their card now they
know not what to believe
We gave them confusion and left them in shame…
In a pillory with their own selves to blame.

They show dander against us - it is themselves they distrust
Beat at their very own game.
They are absolutely furious, insane and delirious:
Victims of their very own frame

Jeer

They can only barely speak to her now because they are

laid to the ground.

They are turned around upside down and her front is turned

to the rear.

Groveling around he cannot hear a sound - his speech was a

trifling jeer.

Now they are enthralled -- hear them call to those whom

had once been their slave.

They pay for the jeer -

With a crocodile tear.

Their answer will come from the grave.

"What's His Names Wife"

They languor and drool all over my lair

with lice and poison ivy all in her hair

She smells of gangrene - putrefied flesh

Giving the senses a shocking distress

He sent his wife to have her wed

Now here she is, she's in my bed

She smells of a stagnant back-water latrine

Now what to do to help her get clean?

Soap and water can't help

She can't even be seen

She had that deep down gut-wrenching emetic decay smell

Something cooked in boiling sewerage. Something dead -

straight from HELL.

She is so putrid - a venomous skunk

Enough to kill a man or make him dead drunk

Now, let his wife with all her charm

Go reside with those Who would cause her harm

Us vs Them

We are aware of their intent
Cover them with a cerement
We know what they try against us
Lock them in the sarcophagus
They are dastardly - and they machinate
Give them back their hate
They work against us to wear us thin
Use it against them: ….jinn
They bring effluvia - it really stinks.
Give them casper - give them jinx
They don't like us because we're here
Make them tremble, make them fear
They come against us - full speed ahead
Make them inert - give them dread.
They use cheap-talk to put us down
Give them the circus - they are the clown
They hurt one another - they walk away sad
They walk away from us - it is us they discuss
When they discuss us - in themselves they do not trust
They say bad things to speak to offend
They wear themselves thin
Get under their skin
They try hard to deceive to offend
Leave them hard - they bend in the end

Betrayed

Get those hebegebees off away from us

We know the tenet of their campaign

Their dependencies are so deep-seated they are obsessed to

seize a claim.

They have developed a need to possess our seed

And when they descry us, they are left perplexed

So they turn to their mirror - in horror in terror

Their images show their rejects

They make themselves believe they have an undying need

to lock themselves inside

Deep into blame, crying in shame

Their souls are dead in their pride

Now they're trying to find someone in time to give them

spark to a new pilot light

They are blind in the dark.

They lied, and betrayed, and they don't feel alright.

Shrewdly desperate, they need a vouch-safe - someone

valid to plead their case

But their habits are adulterated recrudescence, and their

heads are bubbles of intumescence

They need someone to carry their ball - while they escape

You take their fall and even though they promise to pay

You give them their way.

They still betray.

They Don't Mean No Harm

They don't mean no harm

Just want a little attention

Better bring them forth To the stage of life

Before they throw a temper tantrum

But today kept bringing us recurring problems - and we

needed time to resolve them…

But now today will have to wait

The old ancient stuff needs grease

They've been waiting so long - till they cannot be

prolonged

They're about to go phut; they need release

They are hoary; in fame, in legend, in glory.

First in reference; and their exploits must never be

forgotten

They will not be denied -- of their time - travel stride, of

how they did their migration

From the time they died, let them be not belied. But

foretold in reverse immigration.

Countless generations removed away

They want to come to us today

They will need their migration methods recognized

Surely they cannot be seen by naked eyes

In a realm beyond the dead they may be realized

These ancient beings may be spiritized

Thru their progeny they will live new lives

Infusing their spirits they may materialize

Heiroglyphic in their nature, with myth, and theogony in

their theme

They may come and impart to today, what they know about

this scheme

They have been there and they have done that - so they

most assuredly know:

In this fallow, moribund -- entropy of today…which way

man should go.

Yes, they already have the insight to impart to man today:

How to deal with apotheosis; before he is made to stray

If they come from Greek Mythology, which penumbras all

our literature

Today would do well to follow and heed; because today

needs suture and ligature

Battle

They should never have tried to come against us - they had

no reason or rhyme

Now they are denuded of all that they were, including their

place in time.

We don't like having had to speak against them but they

forced us into a battle

Having to fight - spit upon them; spite-freeze them in a

coffin of addle

Paralyze them in all their forms, leave them stinking and

stale

Pour gasoline all over them now, and let them burn in hell

Ill Intentionalisms

They tried to force us into degradation
Their intentions were filled with machinations
Now after so much interrogation
They are moribund with repugnation
Silence their insulting instigation
Give them septicemia impregnation
Because they opposed us with vicious discrimination
We answered them with a hostile elimination

They are a crippled old dog with only one leg
With only one eye lying on its dreg
It will have swallowed its own tongue for not being fed
Pronounce against their attacks! Pronounce against them
dead

No Escape

They weren't satisfied to return to the mud to the swamp

where they all belonged

They were all doped up and filled with lust not knowing

right from wrong

They weren't satisfied to cling to the beetle who provided

them with their dung

We don't let them lick us with their bacteria purulent

tongue…

   like a maddened bloodthirsty King Kong

They all needed to escape their slum and tried to do it

through you

But you would need to shoot your fluid and let your juices

spew

Only then would they be satisfied because then they would

be little you

They were betting on your being blind and dumb and not

knowing what to do

Send them back to where they're from and we will be brand

new

Scape Goat

Seeking a solution to use an ablution to empty his man's

evil heart.

In suicidal sorrow decided to borrow a scheme to start a

new start.

Discard every single one of them, save only just a few.

What sense did it make? The blood is on the take.

It was only transferred but not made new.

Using a shogun to effect a pogrom, the masses is who got

slew.

Searching around for who could be found in the aquatic

strait of the sound,

A fisher of men appeared on the scene to follow his way on

new ground.

Upon closer inspection in their own reflection, now seeing

what they had created.

Images of themselves they found dejection, they berated

themselves whom they hated.

Pass the Buck

So they destroy themselves through the person of you
with a sophistical point of view
clearly knowing not really knowing just what else to do

He hates his dement
and the phut of his intent

For his image was meant to represent –
    a part of himself in vain glorious wealth
But fell short; and plummeted to dissent

Attempting to escape any self-implication
Blame you for your birth as desecration

Lamentation for an Abomination

This is a piece of lamentation
born of hostile discrimination
that followed the melancholy subjugation
of those- so blind to their fault

Lament for the vicious bloodthirsty beast
    whose lockjaw wouldn't let go

Lament for the thief that comes in the night
    whose visits were from below
        and finally got himself caught

Lament, and feel sorry for the criminal ghost
    who thought he'd never be seen

Lament, while he pays the ultimate price
    for being so ugly and mean

Lament, while he begs on his hands and knees
    to return to being a fiend

God and Devil

God and Devil

Who hates whom?

God and Devil

Locked in a room

God and Devil

Archangel Rune

God and Devil

Coming to doom

God and Devil

Wilted in bloom

God and Devil

Conjugated tune

God and Devil

Bride and Groom

God and Devil

Man spoke too soon

What You Say

It has been altered and it has been fixed

It had been broken and cursed with a hex

Now it has been hit in the blink of an eye

Future shock is upon them - from the ground to the sky

Now they will stop their bickering, their petty picayune

Now they will stop their trifling spite or else lose the use of their spoon

Something is coming to attend to your speech and you will be placed in fear

Your geeky challenging efficacious joking will jeer you till you become queer

You will be starving to death without stimulation and be no longer spoon fed

Your careless use of the words in your head will leave your brain brain-dead

Distracted

She left you behind for a reason.
You never looked into her eyes.
Your inclination to her nether region
Is why it is you she despise.
She has pheromones and erogenous zones,
And may be agreeable in estrous.
But your back door approach only brings reproach.
Now the rest of us are being scorned and being jested.
Sure, she looks good and fine and attractive, and maybe
even fetching.
But the manner of your response is repulsive and
depressing,
and surely does leave us wretching.
It was bad enough when you went into heat
and opened your mouth to her bicycle seat.
In your stinking thoughts you were thinking as your twisted
thoughts went adrift
And spittle fell from your slobbering lips
and you said you wanted to whiff;
A she from her bicycle seat

Black circles are brimming surrounding your eyes.
Your lips and eyes have turned red.
Your veins are popping from your neck and your head,
and your pallor looks like it is dead.
Your tongue is lolling with quivering shoulders
and your nostrils are flaring something fierce.
We don't know what to make of you.
You're bringing us all to tears!

The Gamble

At the end of everything is the Letter G.
To frame you into what you can't be
They would toss you around like a pair of loaded dice
And you would define their vice

Depraved and wicked; an immoral churl
They would destroy your world.
Viciously exploiting; drowning you in vice –

First: Apotheosis; then Anti-Christ
No, you CANNOT be their G.

It is not for you.

It is not for me.

Food for Fault

Look at what they made them do
a caveat to us that we must eschew
they were big and brave and mad and bold
disregarding what they'd been told
thinking that they would outdo the best
So she turned and no longer offered her vest
they got relegated to the cistern stool
Effluvia is now what they drool
They made them eat the fecal cake
They are all paying for the same mistake
There's no way for them to escape this mess
They have no way to redress
They have offended something they knew not enough about
To their executioners they prayerfully shout
They hope to be taken into firm embrace
But to the wrong ones they did deface
Slowly being tortured in agonizing pain
They went deep into the drug with nothing to gain
Overcome by panic they run with great speed
Blind with fear they are seeking a creed
They're begging and pleading for the first ones to help
them
But the first ones litter has made them dim
They have been wrought insensate by the defecation
Feeding them what they eat without evaluation
In other words, they don't even let them eat their young
They have given them the beetle – they have given them
the dung
They're trying to keep it a secret that they are all being
hung.

Self-Hate

Black, and ugly, and devilish self-hate is the stuff that ran
through his vein
It was his King. It was his God. It would leave him
withered, bane, insane.
All they do is deceive themselves - nothing else is
important.
They live to live delusion strife - to the limits of all that is
abhorrent.

In his bedroom alone while sitting at home he would please
his nares with a snort.
Someone sold him some warfarin. His nose came up short.
His nasal did distort, but that wasn't his last resort.

His condition - so sadly
He was hooked - so badly
His mind became unhinged.
Five decades of addiction and truth to his conviction,
he faithfully turned to the syringe.

He was made afraid to live his life.
It was a something he hated to face.
He hated the beard and the stress of strife.
He tried to eschew his race.

He hid himself in dark shadows of black below the nether
in his mind.
Enamored and enthralled with the drug of his choice
He could not stop: and made himself blind.

Determined with intent to the greatest extent
to reach a twilight he'd never known before.
He double pumped his needle, singing twiddley-deedle:
and entered a room without a floor.

He felt free-floating in motion with his eyes wide open
In space without stars - all black.
He felt his eyelids close, he felt his body decompose,
and he knew that he wasn't coming back.

Give It To 'em!

Now hit them with a dose of love.

Slice up their verbal assault.

Tongue-tie their hot-headed insult.

They stop their thinking and lose their talk.

They lose their thought, they lose their say.

They lose their means and they lose their way.

They lose track of time – they lose today.

They lose yesterday and they lose tonite.

They lose their head and they lose their sprite.

They lose their gist, and they lose their sway.

They lose their voice, and they lose their play.

They lose direction – they go astray.

They lose their minds with nothing left to say.

From Something into Nothing

They need a whipping boy – a scape goat, someone

pusillanimous;

Maybe a guinea-pig; An inexperienced rustic to make him

feel really big.

They need someone who is gullible, who will not examine

the thought

someone whom they can inveigle. He will think he is

without fault.

They will make him think he is the perfect thing and

everyone is his friend.

They will add to his pride, and he will think - even his fault

has no sin.

They will intumesce his head, blow his mind with

adulation.

Give him false kudo and deliquesce him with inspiration.

They will riddle him with hubris – supercilious will be his.

Guile and duplicity is how they do their biz.

He will vacillate from their twilight, with his head above
the cloud.

In a fugue and delirium; with megalomania ever so proud.

He will be advertised and demonstrated, into universal
fame.

Knowing of their use for him; for him to be their game.

They will have him work as a male factor, a geek and also a
josh.

He will be garrulous and insulting, offending with his bosh.

But he will not understand himself. His rewards are great
and many.

They will ease him into a miasma swamp but he will never
get a penny.

They will eviscerate his mind and even make copies of his
form, yet this is only a scrimmage.

They will take the essences of his countenance and hide

behind his image.

Next will come the battle, they will make him lose his

head.

They will belie him and make him fight against the souls of

the dead.

He will suffer for being complicit, they will fill him up with

dread.

They wish for him to join them. As they are reprobate

to make him become slinky and vile and fill him with their

hate.

He would learn to complain – express bitter blame, joke,

provoke, and instigate.

They will change his name.

He will be sick in his mental vacuity, a loud-mouthed

braggard -in-blame.

Bedecked in splendor and glory; yet specious—insular;

defiled; - and lame.

For all their practical purposes, he will now have become

defunct.

They have molded a "something" into a "nothing" and now

they can use him as junk.

They need him to play in a key-stone role, so they gave him

the vox popu-li;

In niggling subterfuge and clandestine stealth, he would be

their cretin; vivifying their biggest lie.

He would be paltry, extant, excoriating; and full of swill,

Pulsillanimous, excreta – and without his own will.

Now they begin to gormandize him. His condition is so

delicious.

The games they played to gain control of his mind, were

heinous and mercilessly vicious.

Now they begin to inveigle him – butter him up with their swill.

To make him proud and arrogant and get him under their will.

Embellish him in shining colors and crown him in glorified praise.

And yet, if he remains too gullible, he will stay in a nebulous maze.

If he recognizes his persecutions, he will recognize his plight.

If he discerns that he is now a victim, he may retaliate with a fight.

They adulate him to make sure for them that he gets all the attention.

They need him to think that he is all of everything so they can hatch the plot of their intention.

They offer him the dope, and the smoke, and the pill; and

the sensuous vices that give pleasure

They offer him dreams of ecstasy, of joys beyond any

measure.

They need him groomed and conditioned: as a paradigm to

act on the stage of the world.

To play a part that is specious – yet, he would be seen as a

churl.

They would cause him to become a simile; by subterfuge

and pseudonym.

Having the grandizing image of an Apotheosis rune –

yet, in the nether of the gilt of the image, noting more than

a loon.

Now he begins to think to himself; sitting in his four-

cornered room.

How can he reject their influences upon him? Sending him

to his doom?

So he thought through his dilemma and he thought while he

was asleep.

He thought until he realized it: That they were playing him

cheap.

He kept thinking till he came to an epiphany: they were

intending to ruin his name

Cause him to become procumbent – deluded – debased –

along with profaned!

He dropped his obtuse; caught on to their ruse and named

the tune of their game.

They went into an epilectic seizure, a grand mal catatonia!

They were gripped by a catastasis – followed by aphonia.

It happed so quickly – in the blink of an eye! It was a

shock, stunning and sudden!

It took them by surprise, their hair stood on end, they ran to

hit the panic button.

They knew not what to do – they caught diarrhea, and

catalepsy too.

While they were inert, they were also inept, they could not

materialize.

Now he would take advantage of them, and peer into their

eyes.

He beheld and what he saw nearly threw him into a tizzy.

It staggered his senses and left him feeling dizzy.

He saw every disease known to man and every sorrow,

every woe.

Then he saw his very own face and that is what let him

know -

Through his own image he saw a hateful foe.

He saw their guile; he saw their vile. He could smell their

paltry breath.

Effluvium, dung and the vomited products of decayed

death.

This was not recondite; this was not abstruse.

He only had to drop the twilight and put his brain to use.

If he could only transcend his period of decline he could

liberate his very own mind.

Dream states in waking life now began to appear.

A lucidity distilled itself – clearing his atmosphere.

Out from under being insensate his brain began to click.

He brought himself to understand why they were making

him sick.

They had been staring at him, studying him, and found him

perfect for their use.

With charm and malfeasance and murderess deliberation,

They would entice him to fall for their ruse.

But their harassing instigation, and constant prestidigitation

shed light on their equivocation.

They were dissembling, temporizing, and full of

machination.

If he had fallen into their trap, he would become an

everlasting sap

The greatest humiliated fool; a cretin, a churl.

A perfect pusillanimous dummy – a perfectly mindless

tool.

And now he would let them be shard. He would give them

unto the bard.

The bard would sing of their plot of what they intended to

do

It was discovered because of the mistakes they made.

They were erratic and deceptive too!

Dystopian in their view, in panic-stricken conniption fits,

they point blame at one another.

In a paradigm of an age-old scheme – to turn one against

the other.

That's what they were working against him.

But, alas, he wasn't so dim.

Recruited to believe in their ill-founded creed, would be his

death sentence – indeed.

If they could make him believe what he could not conceive,

they would conquer him as an invention.

Set against creation to serve them in their contention.

The grand major deception is exposed. Through the bard,

and the song, and the prose.

They failed to make him think he was prince, an

underworld apotheosis.

They failed to make him think he was above; Lord of Hosts

– and Lord of Hostest.

They are ripped apart and shred to shard, and likely not to

recover.

As to chances to begin again – they will not receive

another.

He latched onto their scheme in the nick of time to not fall

into their jin.

Avoiding being blinded – and drowning in vice, glorified in

all their sin.

He did escape the rant of their change to invent him into

their God.

But they broke their own nefarious hearts: they failed after

trying so hard.

They had needed his personage to hide behind to go against

their foe,

By sending him into an oblivion; trying to deliver a blow.

He would had thought he was something – yet he would

had been nothing.

And that's how the story did go.

The Thirds

They don't want to accept the things being said –
It's too incredible. They could lose their head.
It's too deviant for them to conceive.
That's why we don't tell them what to believe.
There are reasons why you hear only a one-sided story.
The main character praises his very own glory.
His character is directed toward his megalomania credit.
You hear very little about his shortcoming debit.

He is multi-faceted in name and rune.
But now that he is mad you will see his buffoon.
He stayed too long on a hostile track
He got hung-up on a hate-trip, and couldn't turn back.
All for himself he made all the rules.
Within himself he made himself lose
His only presentation is himself as a tier – two-thirds of
himself is to generate fear.
The first one-third was given to appear
To act as a sacrifice – whose job was to steer
By speaking in riddles – leaving meanings unclear.

The second one-third was supposedly the pate.
To save all of you from the evil and the hate.
But the evil and the hate benighted the pate.
It divided the triune: and made them separate.
With all his selves and names and runes,
They got mixed up inside, playing too many tunes.
The third one-third, the evil and the hate,
Benighted the second one-third, the pate.
They falsified themselves through anger and hate.
Dooming themselves to fate.

He kept refusing to share with his ugly side any credit,
glory or fame.
All he could think of was glorifying his name.
So they all go down the same drain.
Their spouses cannot speak up for them.
They can't sing them an encouraging song.
They cannot parade them and help them be strong.
They know they are broken and ashamed of themselves.
They know they have all done wrong.

Hubris

They don't know what's wrong with them.
They never figured it out.
They all played the hero's part.
Now they are full of doubt.

They are the ones who defied the world.
Seeking fortune and fame.
They chose to fight the deified nature.
Now they're put to blame.

Everything is wrong with them.
Every ailment included.
They're so blind they see no shame.
Like lepers, they stay secluded.

They think to be something they cannot be,
To transcend to a higher ground.
They speak the tongue of the murky swamp,
Searching for what is never found.

Whatever they claim to believe in,
The place their own ego first.
But because they learn to deceive so well,
They stay empty, dying of thirst.

But they were big and strong and they thought so much,
They thought too much of their self.
They thought they were more so than those who brought
them,
They were stored on a pantry shelf.

It got took away from then what they were made of;
From a whisper to a raging roar.
Now they pray from one fathom down,
To entice to start another war.

Lost Love

From one to another of like kind and mind.

If we don't defend we will lose our time.

If we lose our time, what good would it had done,

For mother and father to had dragged us along?

To see us play dead and lose their throne.

To lose our letters from the bees to the Z's.

And lose their love and be left alone.

And we would be lost, and them dead and gone.

The End of It

Hanging from a tree limb by a hook in his nose
Whose tip is piercing his head.
His feet are still kicking and his heart is still ticking,
But his brain is assuredly dead.
Evil in his nature can't keep being spread.

They have certainly lost their head.
Let's not wait for them to try to make a comeback.
Let's just give them a catalytic attack.

They have no head and their forces are scattered.
They have no fighting spirit.
And their bodies are battered.

Now let's relegate them to the dead.

Don't Fall Behind

It seems to us for all you know, you don't know what to do.
You follow behind their every whim, act out their every
clue.
They gave you swill and leftovers, and bones and slop.
And the dead leaves from age-old crops.
And you follow behind their blinding speed and don't
know when to stop.
They drink your blood and swallow your genes, and fail
you in your flop.
Interregnum.
Moratorium.
All of everything – stand still.
Invisible confusion is the word of the day.
Directed against your will.
You needled us with poison – pills and smoke and
venom…
Chemicals and nuclear medicines, and fruits as sour as
lemons.
Don't you see what they're trying to do? To turn you
toward her poo?
Trying to make you do what he did. To use her ass as quid.
She did that to him cause his dirty filthy grime, cause they
be so wrong in their frat.

They always come up with a trick-in-a-scheme, while
hiding behind a rat.
He is the one who made the statement, so loudly, so clear,
and so bold.
He said that she was "looking so good" he would eat her
what?
Staring at her behind.
Don't follow those people everything they are about, they
want you too to be blind.
Now this took place a long time ago, when up her ass went
his head.
The first and last word excreta comes out of their mouth – a
habit of speech,
For what they are fed.
Their mouth is full of S--- and that's the first word they
spit.
But don't follow their lead in the conniption-fit say:
Talking S--- may be the predator to make you their prey.
We don't go behind them – they don't lead us astray.

Something Better

He spoke a few words about 'his first three'.

All he said was "My First Three".

To me it was a decry between themselves and TV

To the last three, it isn't going that way.

This pen has the final word and say.

The curse has been lifted.

We will stay clear and free.

We don't have the drugs and vice and perversions and hate.

Our minds are not ruined with diseases reprobate.

We're not stuck in the mud and down in the drain.

We're not gullible, and vile, insane in shame.

The curse has been lifted and so have we.

We have someplace else to go and something better to be…

On Death

Scrub their crud off of us, and, dispel their heebegeebe.

We don't appreciate that they scoff at us, as they use their accursed Ouija.

We have nothing to do with them, shun their overall plan.

They may be called "The Misanthropic" to destroy the minds of man.

As a misogynist they go around foaming:

To bring harm to the mind's of the woman.

How shall we defend ourselves? And who should we beseech?

To not be thrown into their hell – to escape their blood-sucking leech?

Tell us the reasons for our being here, what purposes do we serve?

To learn the fright – to fear something? Only to lose our nerve?

Blood and guts, and skin and bone, the body is really the real.

When it is dead and gone, maybe buried in the ground.

Has it become some other creature's meal?

So they worry us to death – to hasten – to end our breath.

To enjoy themselves another meal.

Or get you to kill one another, either way it goes…

If you come from a mother your fate is already sealed.

Don't Do It

They want badly to fight us.

They are swill and detritus.

We shall reduce to the size of a flea.

We know they will berate us.

Because we know us, they hate us.

They want to be like you and me.

In the size of the flea.

And with the weapon of the bee.

And the strength of the elephant beetle.

We will use the angry mosquito.

With its hypodermic needle.

And then bite them with the infamous tsetse.

We will use a hemipteran to finish them off.

And a nematode or trematode or two.

We make them tremble to meet us.

They know they cannot defeat us.

We leave them livid, black, and blue.

Not Broken

They say we are phylum from the same tree,
according to the classification.
But we're not like them no matter what,
they carry too much falsification.
They go around belying us,
jaw jacking and betraying trust.
They came running amok with insulting joking,
and trifling and deceit.

Trying to change us into what they are,
something broken- defining defeat.
All the things they've tried against us,
we never let them prevail.
All the things they've said against us,
lock them in their own jail.

They challenged our life to waste our time.
Let's bring an end to their life and waste their mind,
and leave all that trash behind

Let Me Educate You

Now I'm addressing directly to you,

to obstruct your going askew.

So those who need you duped and confused,

can't penetrate your parse point of view.

Gratis - except your own sesqui.

So don't let them do you hegemony.

Construct your own defensive phrase,

Be voluble to retort, your own vista report,

And leave them in a twilight of a haze.

It's a cold war of speech - palaver-

intercalating between the lines.

Designed to blind your hearing and raise your dander,

so that your cogitation will falter behind.

They work the negatives against your innocence,

to make you sleepy and lame.

Then instill fear using sugar-coated jeer,

to rape the slate of your brain.

They are strongly attracted to keep you distracted,

to the theme of sex and aggression.

They use subliminal suggestion to turn your direction,

toward flushing you into a drain.

Bypass their time-wasting friction.

Eschew their pharmacological addiction.

Dazzle them back with an aggregate of colloquial,

And counter their hostile fiction.

Let us fill those empty brain cells of yours

so you won't be used as prey.

So, when they come around to play on your ground,

you will know just what to say.

A Prayer too...

Our Czar who thwarted Heaven

Hollow-head be thy name

Thy King is wrong

Thy will be gone

And we see you're all insane

Give us this day for us to play

We pray to cast you away

We wish to harass and destroy your past

And with us you will never again stay

We will forgive and you are forgotten

For you are the sin

And you are the rotten

And forever may you ever stay away.

Bleach Their Shit

Bleach their debris
strife
Bleach their espri
life
Bleach their house
head
Bleach their mouth
dead
Bleach their eyes
hag
Bleach their spies
stag
Bleach their hair
heed
Bleach their air
deed
Bleach their teeth
trite
Bleach their speech
fight
Bleach their chief
form
Bleach their jeer
storm

Bleach their

Bleach their

Bleach their

Bleach their

Bleach their

Bleach their

Bleach their

Bleach their

Bleach their

Bleach their

Bleach their

Bleach their

Bleach their seer
walk
Bleach their spite
talk
Bleach their sight
skin
Bleach their hate
kin
Bleach their spate
sin
Bleach their heed
hole
Bleach their geed
soul
Bleach their jeeze
hearing
Bleach their sleaze
jeering
Bleach their chi
insistence
Bleach their tree
existence
Bleach their eyes
Bleach their lies

Bleach their

Bleach their

Bleach their

Bleach their

Bleach their

Bleach their

Bleach their

Bleach their

Bleach their

Bleach their

Bleach their

The thoughts don't show the conscious brain activity
processes that should manifest outward cogitation.

The atmospheres are without currents of electrical brain
wave activities.

Instead, the atmospheres appear to indicate a vacuity filled
with instinctive emotional insinuations.

Insect Defense

I will not let you abuse us.
Those who are bonded to me
I won't let you exploit, misuse, or accuse us
As if we had no liberty
We will not let you defame us
As we know you're trying to blame us
For your foilables -you can't see

We're no parts of your reprobation
Of your demented and decay-filled will
You yourselves went against all the grain
To give yourselves a thrill
We're not joining your entourage
To push a boulder up the steep of a hill

You created your own hell on Earth, joking!
Being a mischievous geeky cuss – don't try to blame us!
Because you went wrong – you can't put the blame on us!
You came to us with disrespect, as if you had a right
Do you really think we would mitigate you to alleviate your
plight?
No! Return to excremental swill and septicemia blight.

Now We Put the Hurt on You

Now we put the hurt on you,
and feed you to the dogs.
The way they did Jezebel.

Now we put the hurt on you,
In the pig sty – as slop for the hogs
Through their entrails
And send you straight to hell

Now we put the hurt on you,
To break your teeth, and shut your mouth
And sentence your soul to jail.
We will throw you down so you will never be found
And your eye and speech will fail.

Now we put the hurt on your mind
A terrible thing to waste
Relieve you of your demented thoughts
And leave your life erased.

Be a Little High

You offer us a conflict, we offer you a spar.

Take this epitasis, you won't get very far.

Better for you than sublimaze, ecstasy or meth,

Come palaver with us in parlance.

We will relieve you of your breath.

But, why should you care if you lose your speech?

Your argot is tripe anyway.

You were asked a hundred times to control your tongue.

You let the drugs get in the way.

We really don't want to give up on you

But you made a lot of people get mad

So we thought it best to excoriate you

And give you this jeremiad.

You hold us in umbrage and we hold you in scorn

Because you gave in to the dregs

You have lost your mind from the top of your head to the
lower ankle parts of your legs

Then, you began to be a nobody, a churl, a rustic, a goon

In a downward spiral at the speed of sound, a complete and
absolute loon

So don't complain to us about your foilable

You made your own life unenjoyable.

Surprise!

My mouth starts to water and the air is getting hotter

As I watch the tiny body of a kid it's hard not to pounce

     -But it sways with a jounce

......Stay put

      -I've got to stay hid.

Just let it keep walking so it don't detect my stalking

This one is a really nice quid.

Need a lonely country road, where the school house is old,

Where the traffic isn't crowded and gritty.

But no. Think about today, right here in the city.

In fact, some of them are really quite pretty.

My eyes begin to itch, and I know they must be red.

Sweat begins to drip…

But I mustn't lose my head.

NOW!! Get closer to it now, while the traffic isn't dense.

Offer money and candy. Hope it has no sense.

Smile to it – grin – show it BIG - WHITE – TEETH.

Act real friendly with loving invitation.

Now that's a professional thief.

Show it the candy…

"Hey! Hop on in! I'll give you a ride!

We'll have fun on the way"

That's what kids like – 'fun on the way'

Like squirrels – appearing to play all day.

But this isn't play, from my point of view

I've got something to do.

The kid opened the door, set the book-bag on the floor,

And blithely scooted up onto the seat.

I smiled to myself as a pat on the back.

Life can really be sweet.

Large brown eyes were checking me out,

As I turned to glance into a mirror.

The kid reached into it's book bag and toward me,

Slid an inch or two nearer.

Now here we are at cruising speed,

And in my mirror I smile a sly grin.

I glance at the child sitting next to me,

Holding a real hand grenade --- without the pin.

Desire

They will see her dark and surly secrets

her life in the stinking mud.

They will see the lies in her eyes

and the sin in her grin

and the sickness in the blackness of her blood.

They will see the slither in her dither

as she beckons you hither.

You know she's up to no good.

Hear her gurgling speech.

Through dripping phlegm she beseech

To beguile you with her voice,

to sway you as her choice.

To be home with her alone,

to feed her sucking leech.

Her slimy eyes are open now -

Half-seeing and shining red,

glazed over and crossed,

And showing mad and hate,

from a life of drugs and dregs.

Yes, it is you, her object of derision,
of whom she has made a decision -
to bag herself a big one,
a wealthy healthy slick one,
to occupy her bed.
Look closely and see her quaking,
sweating with shoulders shaking.
A vivacious indication to pronounce
she isn't faking her intentions,
and she sees you as prey.

Self Medicated

They saved your mommy and daddy
their necks from the rope
but who's going to save your child and grandchild
from the smoke, the pill, and the dope?

Medical hemp is what they call it.
Oil from the flower and the leaf
Great grandchild of the Lotus,
With chemicals to give you grief.
But you will not know that you're grievous
or that your brain is impaired.
Anesthetized and numbed to the bone,
you don't feel the pain, so you're not scared.

Vengeance

Because you broke our children's hearts with
> Insouciance and cold-hearted malice.
We're going to burn down your dog-house,
> And then burn down your palace.
Because you ordered us behind you, to follow
> In the wake of your spores.
We're going to eviscerate your thought activities,
> And rob you of your stores.
Because of how you treated us…with black death
viciousness,
> And left us out in the cold,
We're going to make you look like you were
> Two thousand five years old.
You treated us with such a hateful contempt,
> Till we still tremble today.
You're the ones who made us hate ourselves,
> We will punish you without delay.

Because you left your mark on us,

> We will do what we must do.

In a never-ending gauntlet,

> You will hear the stentorian shrew.

Now you will have no safe house,

> Nor shelter or any place to hide.

We will counter your invasion and niggle you with
abrasion.

> You will have no place to reside.

We are a parasite upon your psyche because of the tyke

> whom you treated so cold and so cruel.

We will batter your organ of corte

> Because you relegated us to the stool.